STAR COLORING BOOK

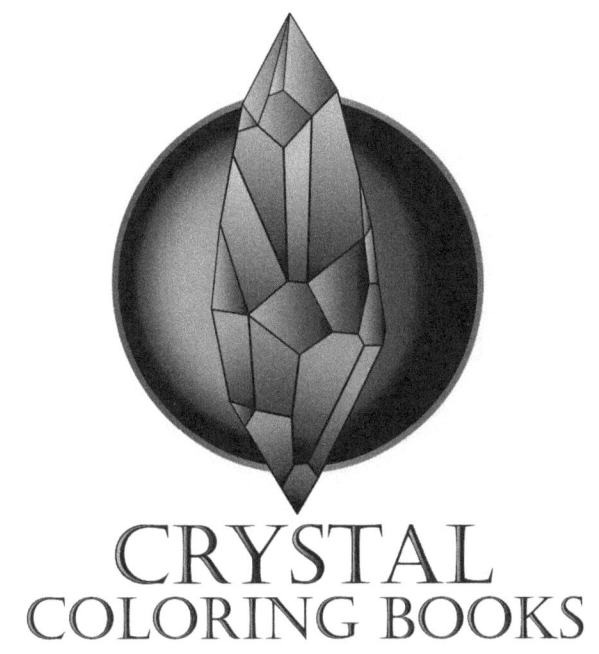

CRYSTAL
COLORING BOOKS

ISBN-13: 978-1984003607

ISBN-10: 1984003607

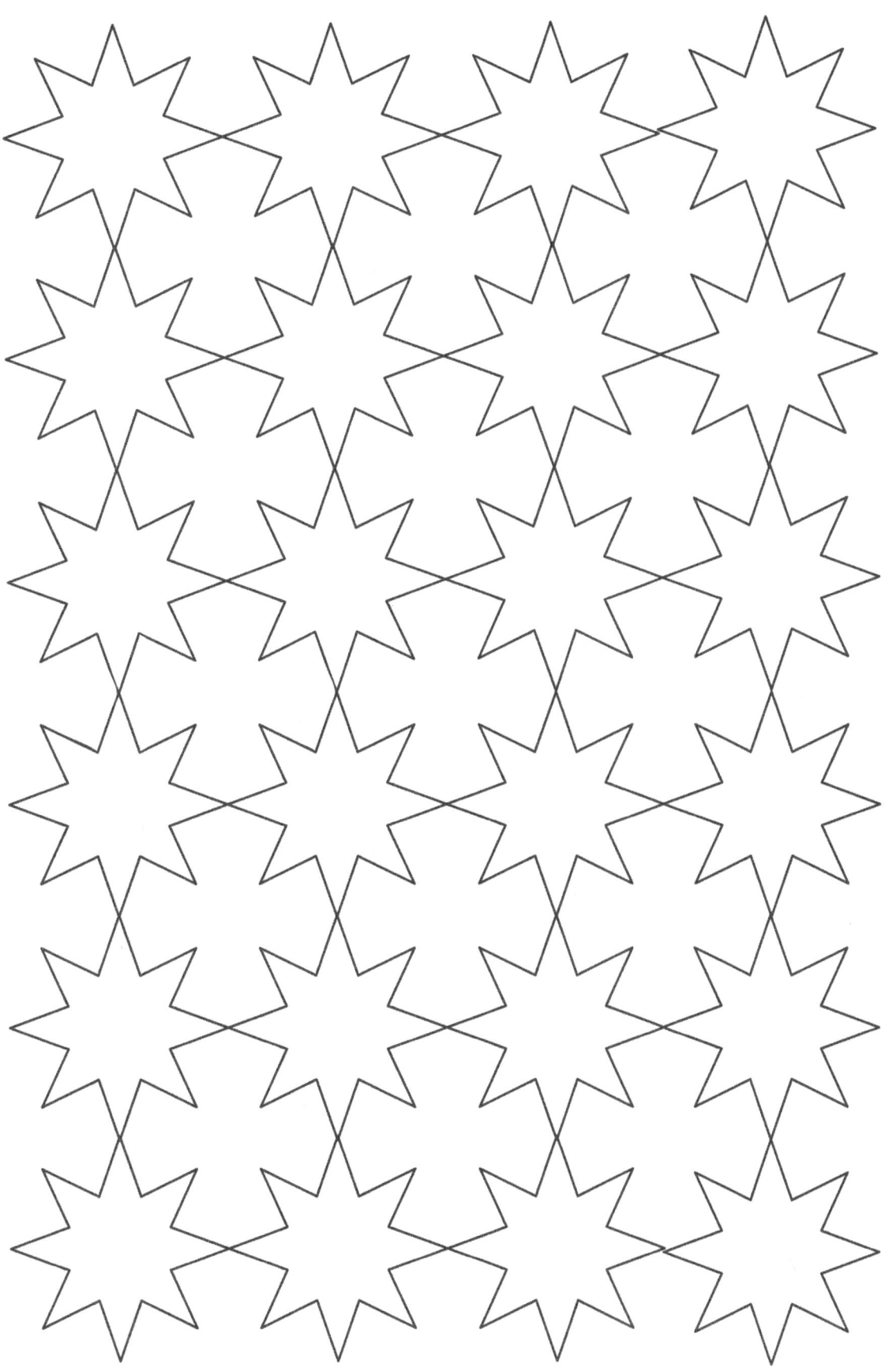

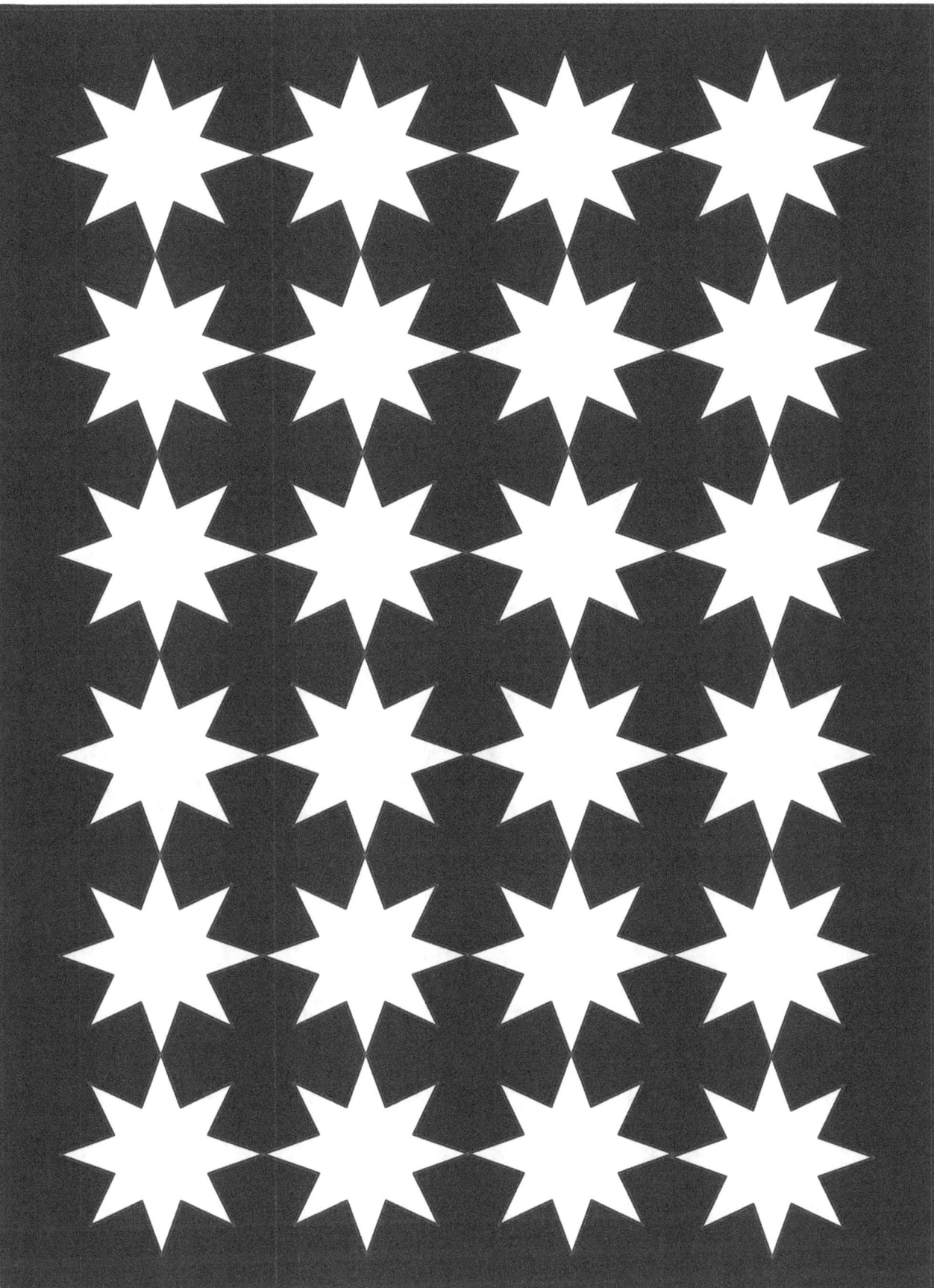

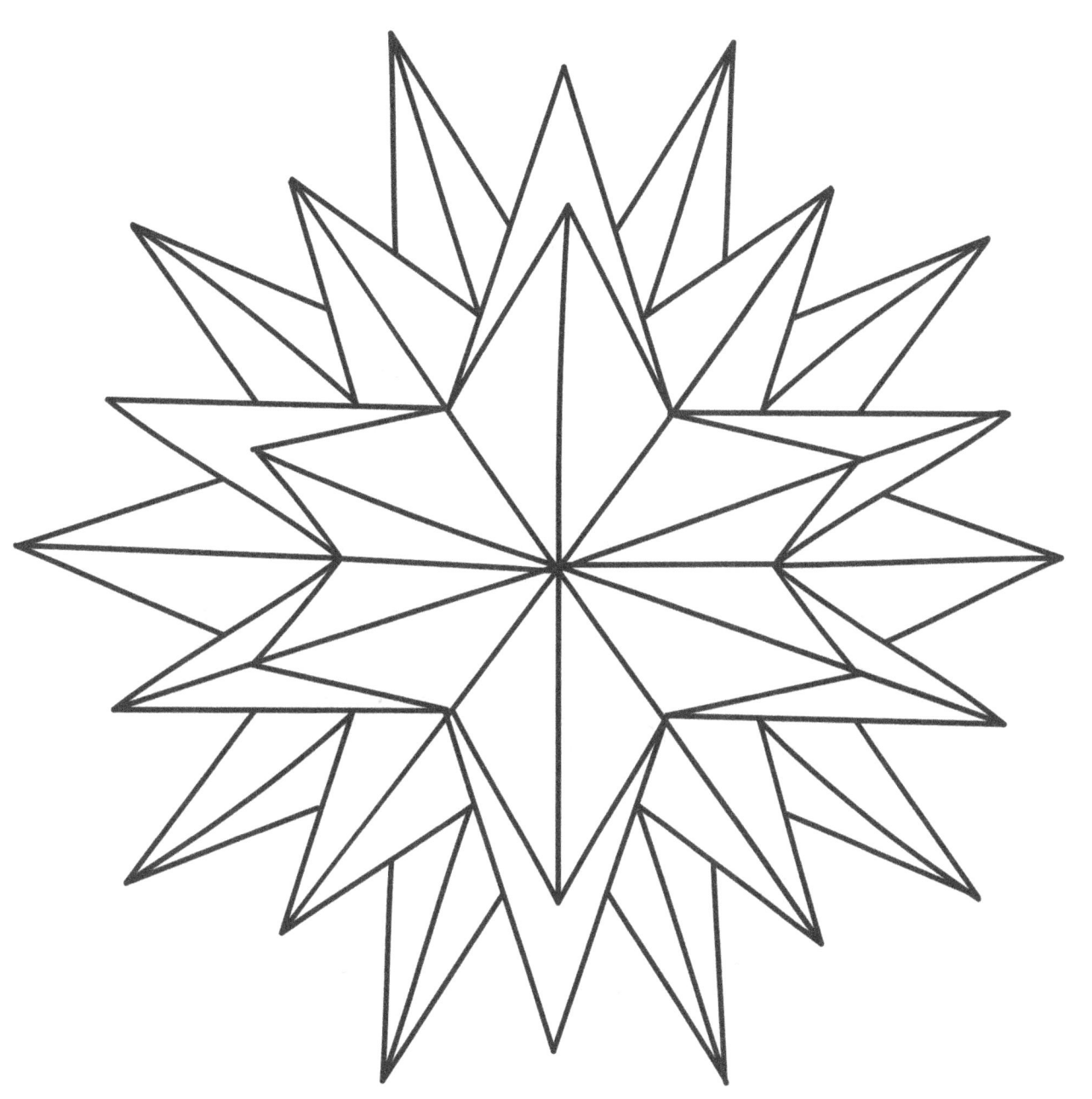

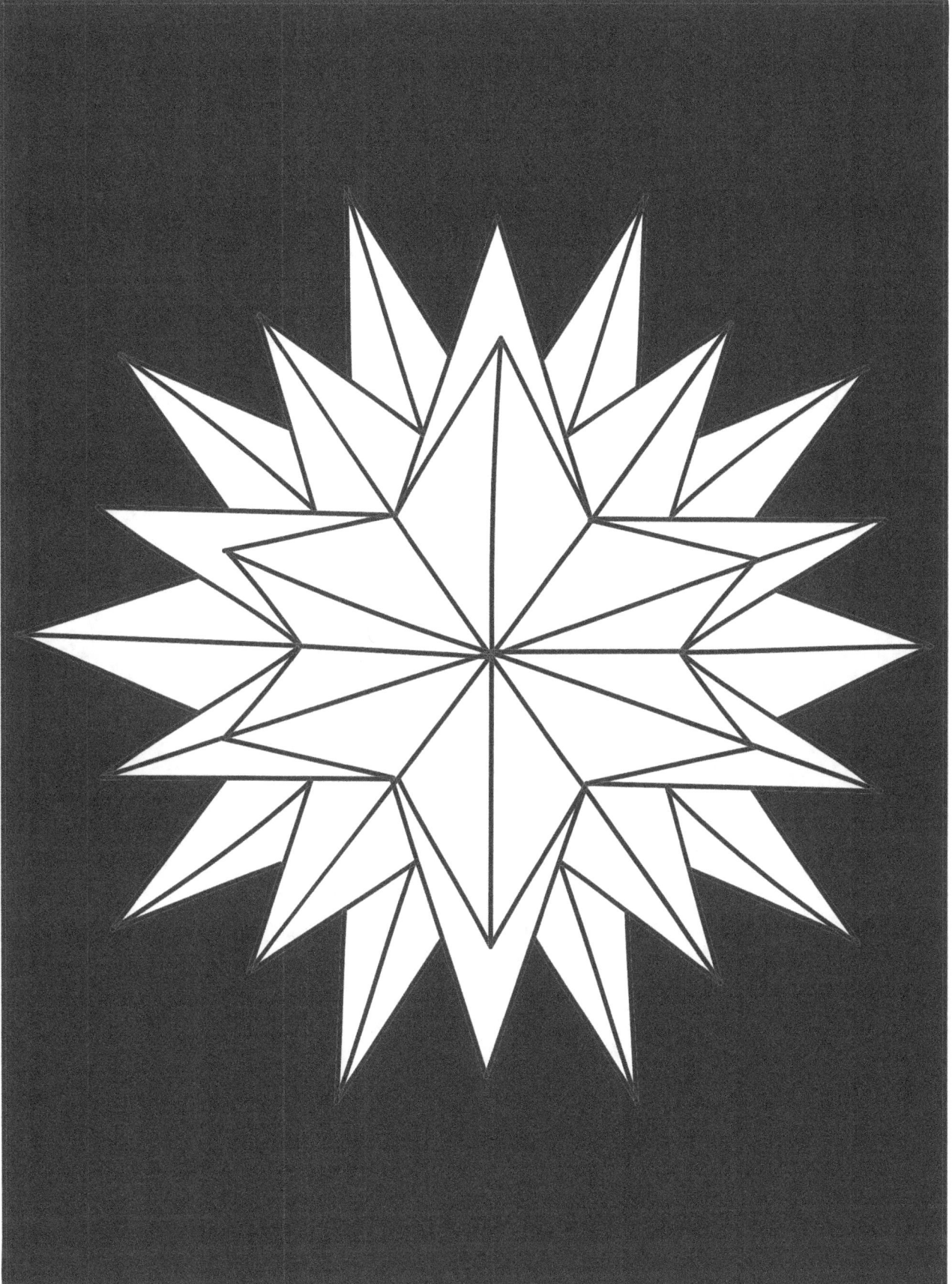

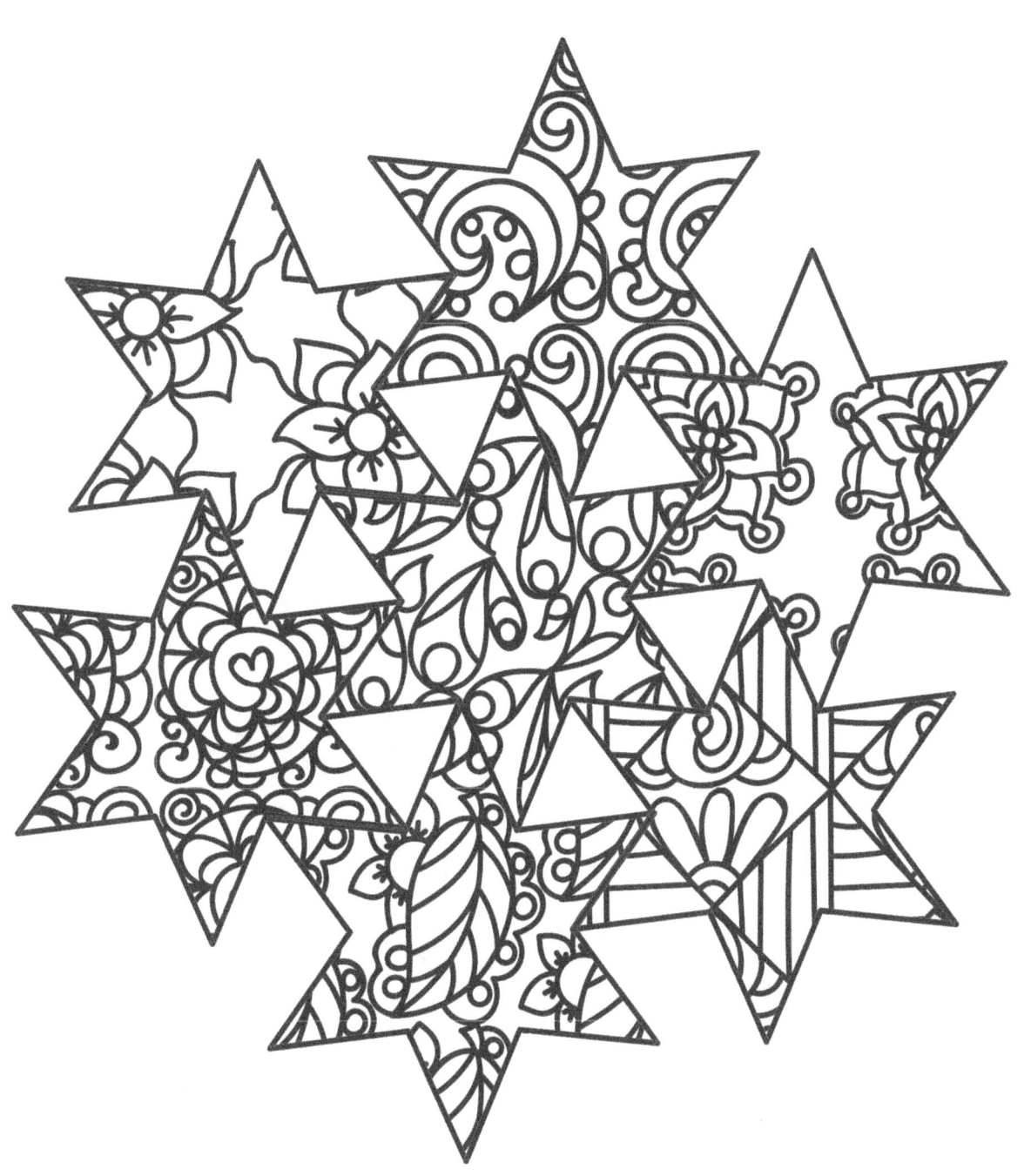

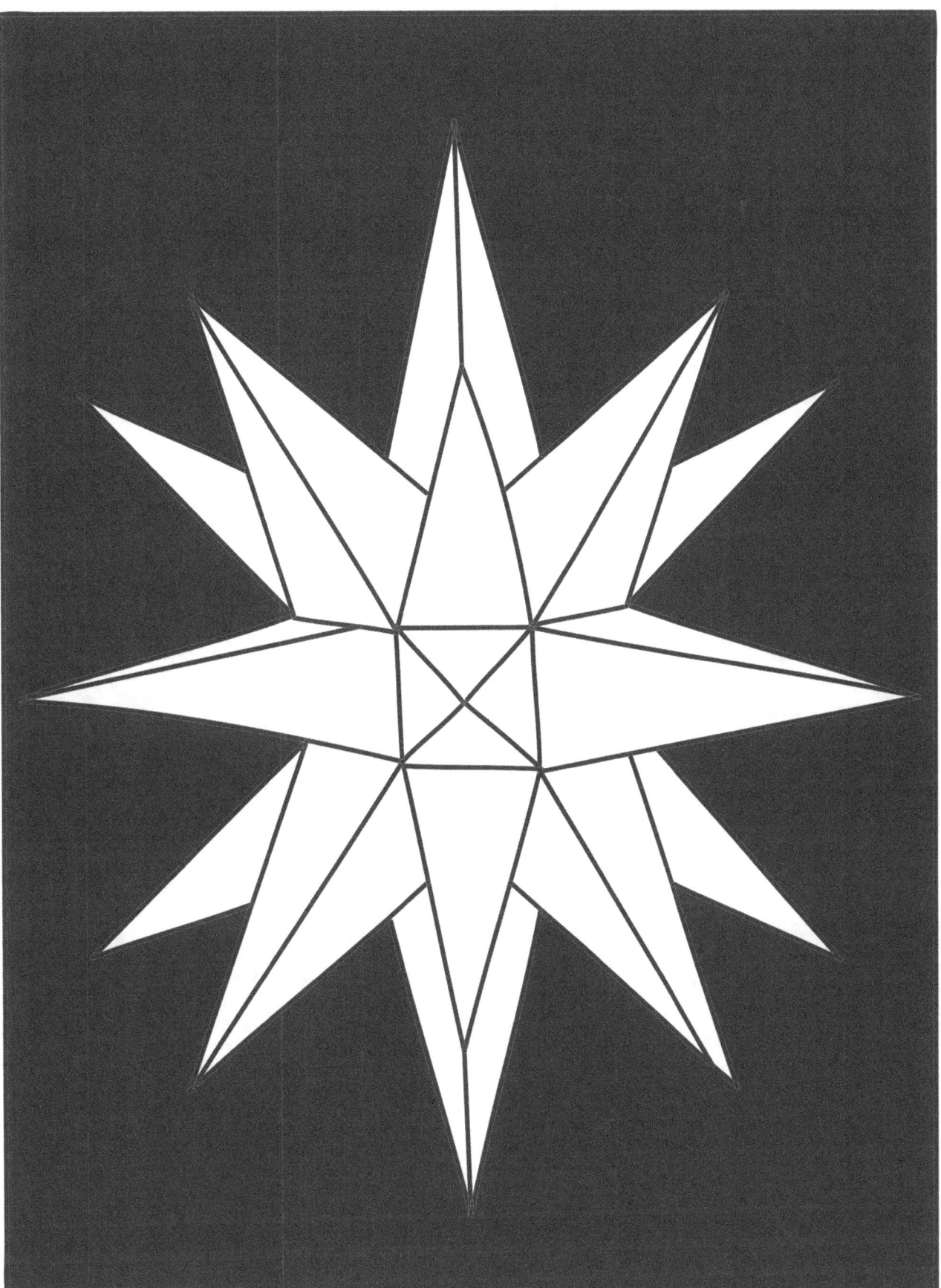

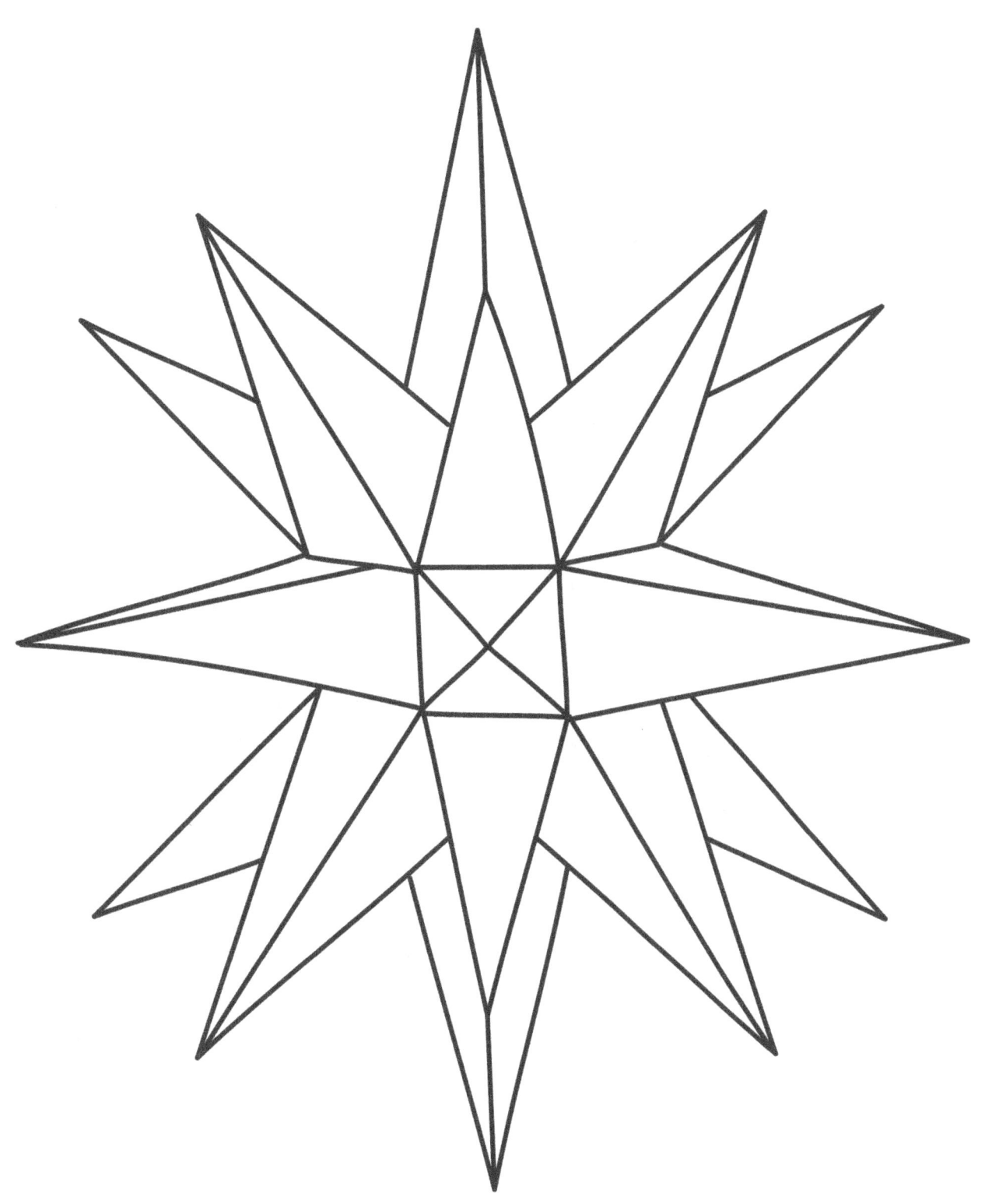

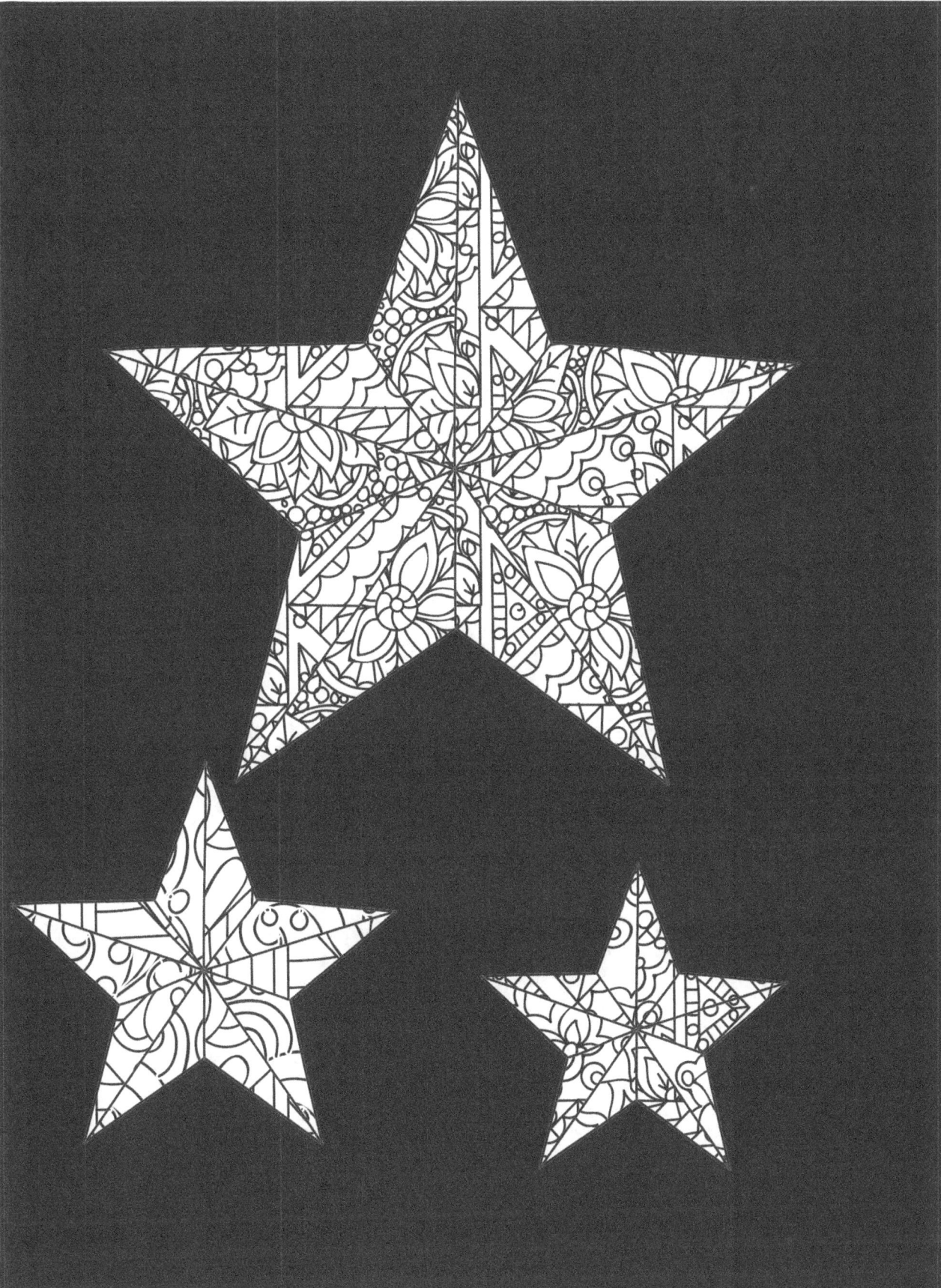

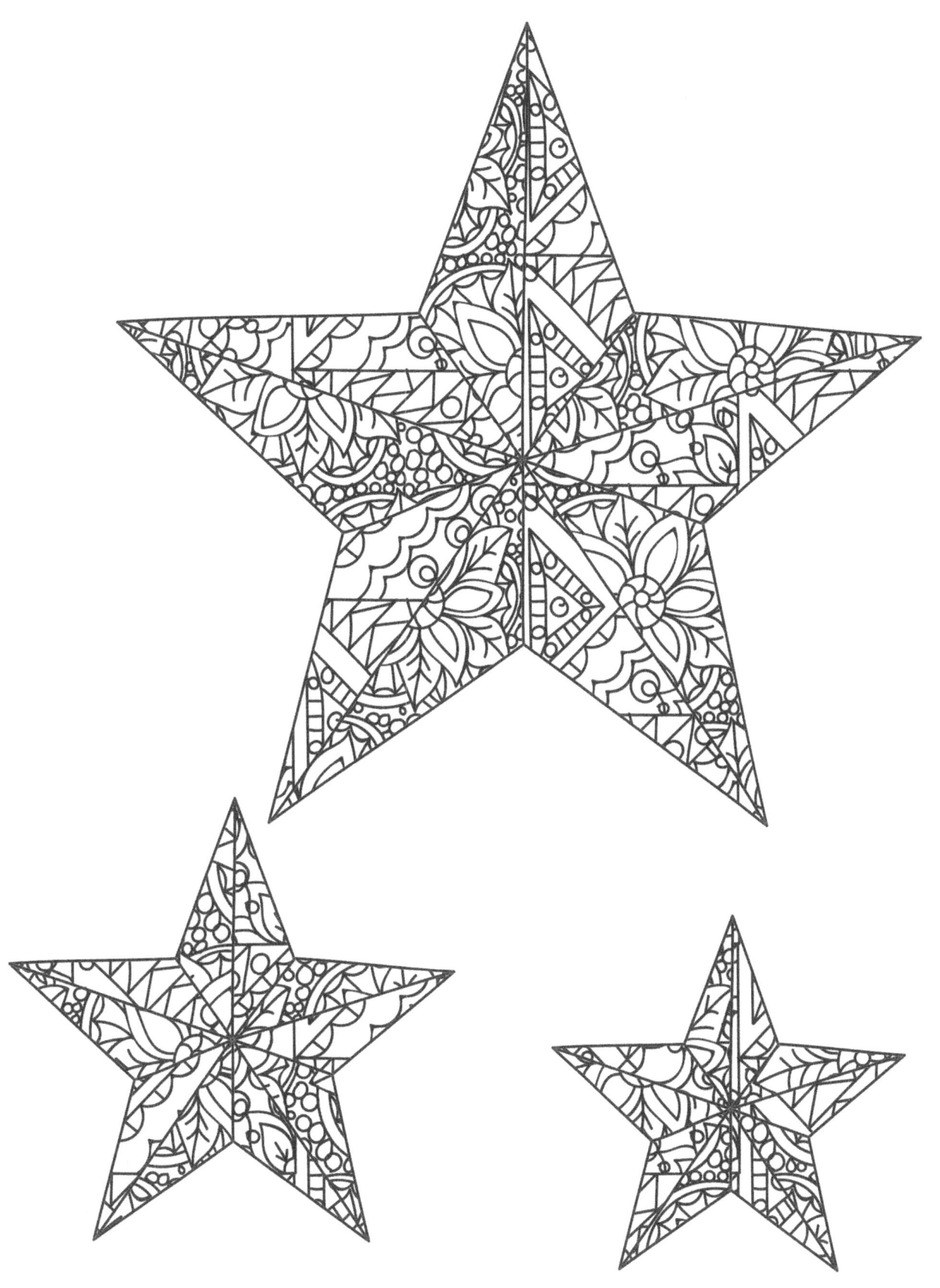

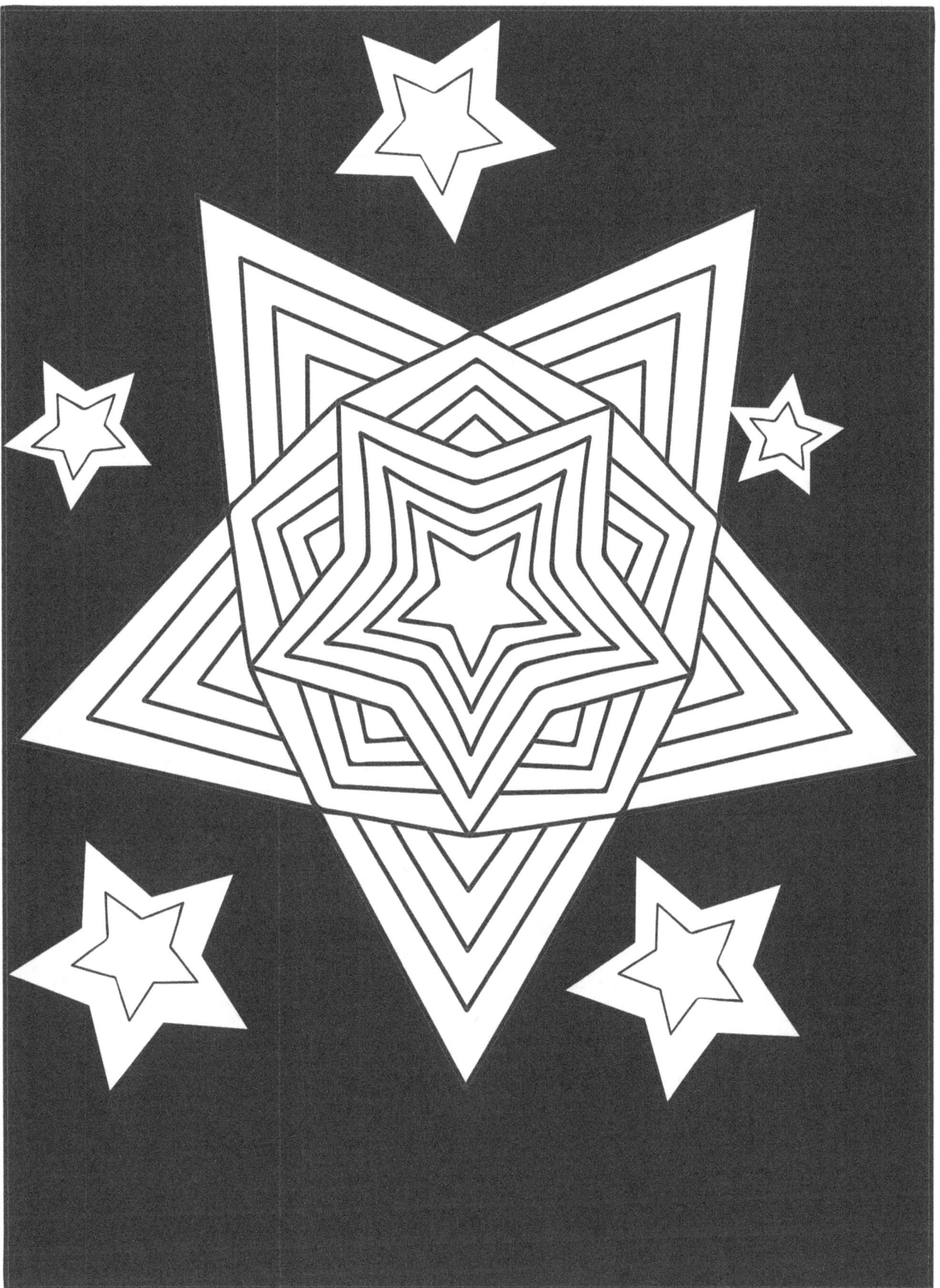

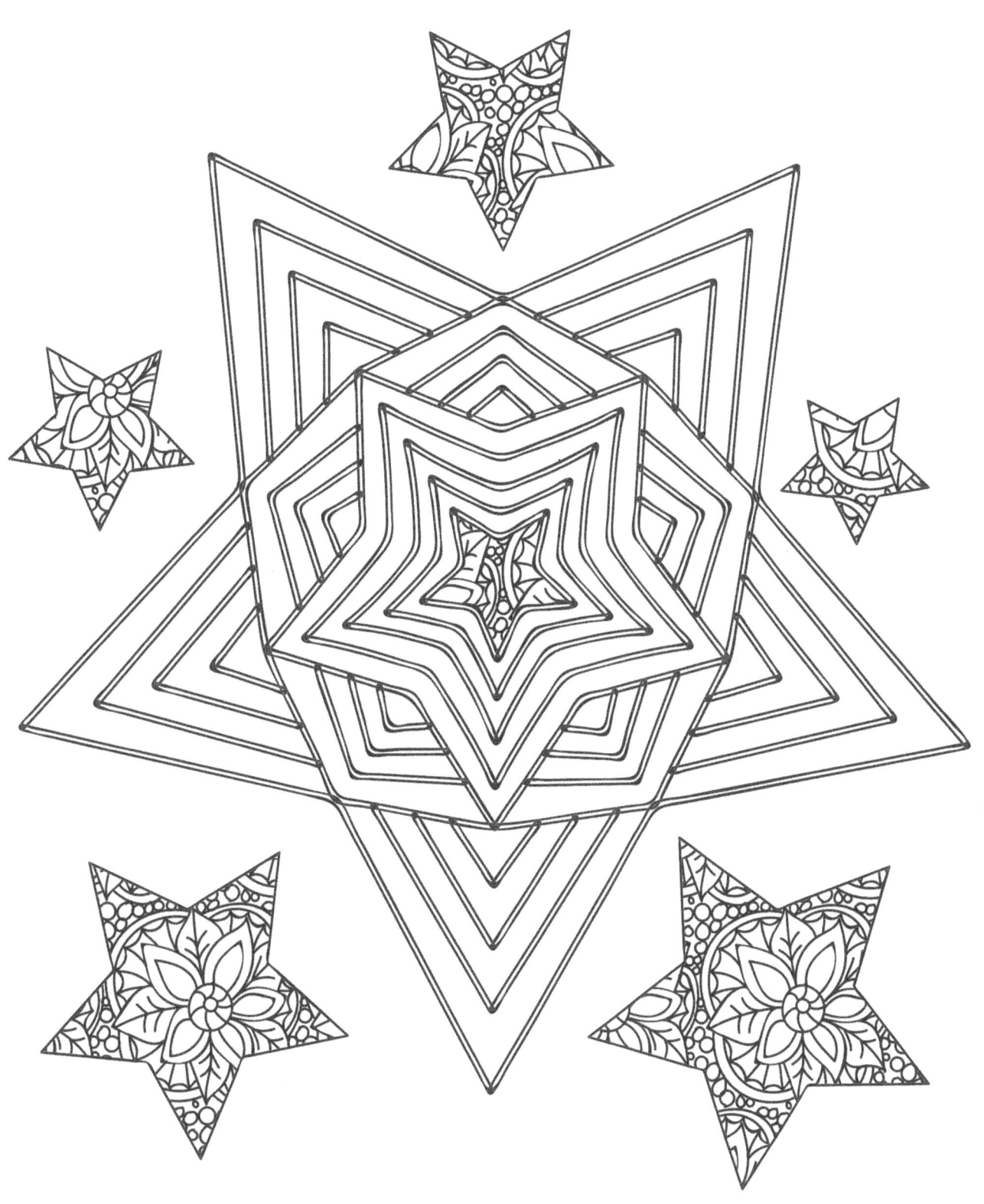

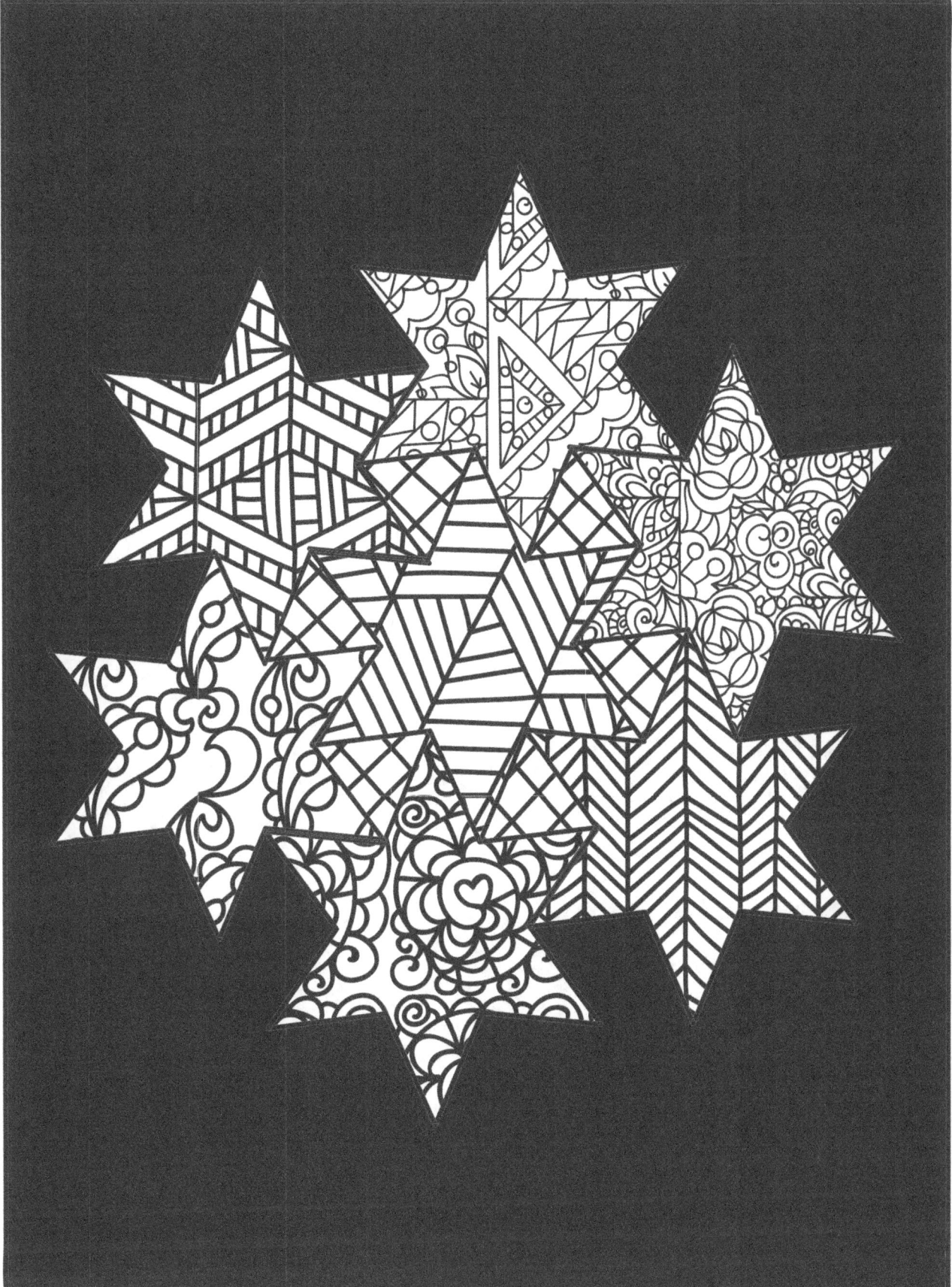

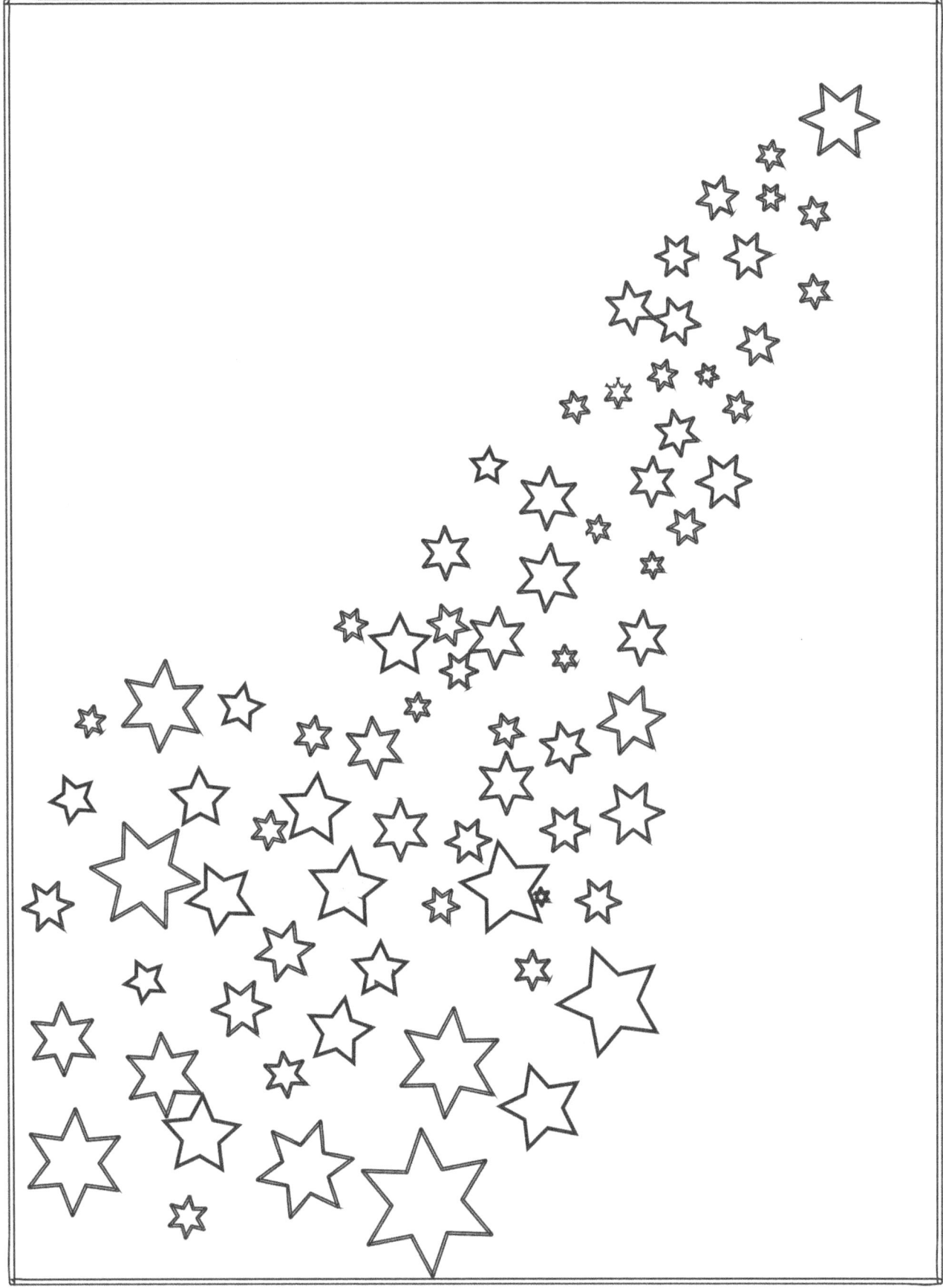

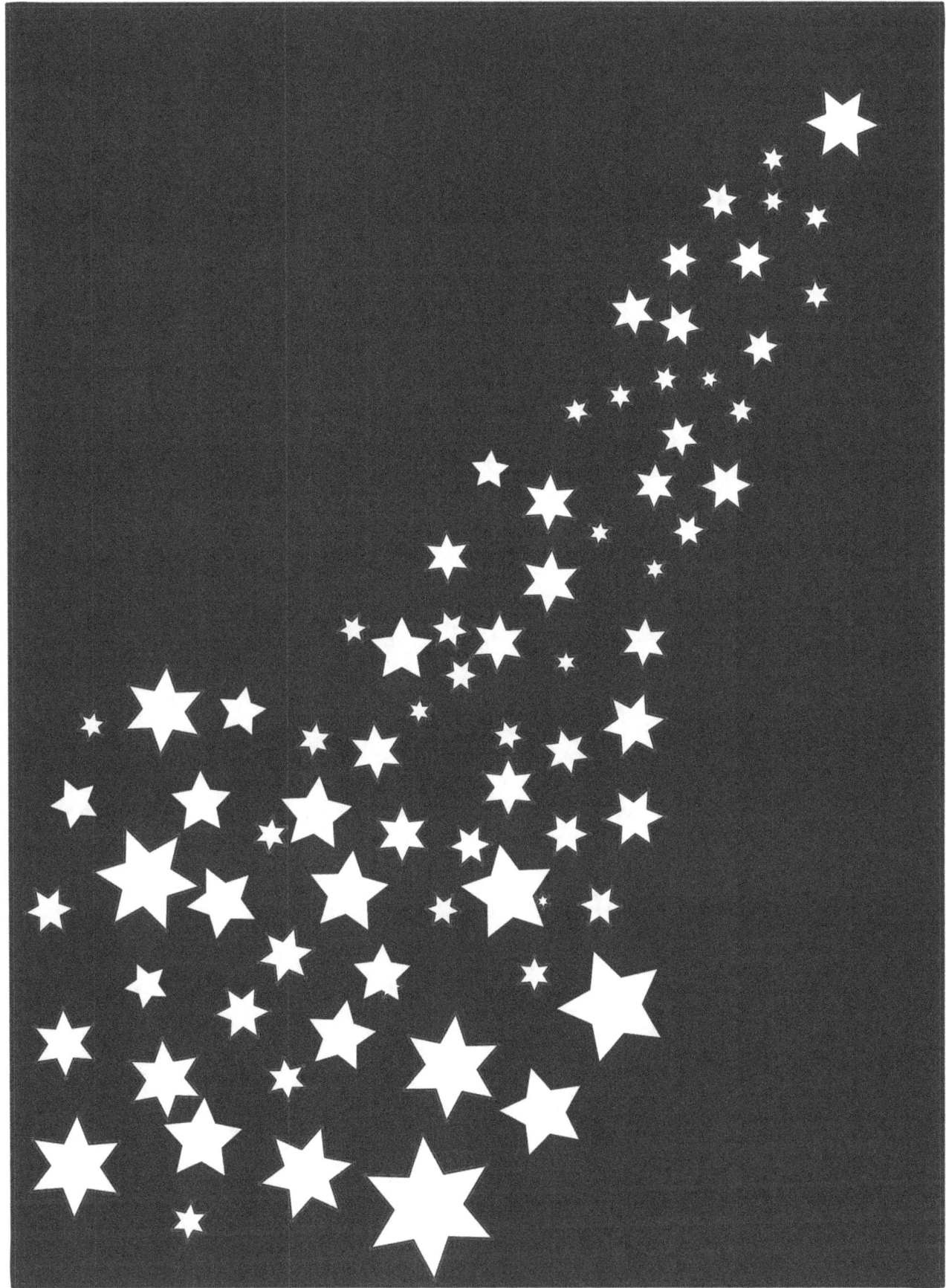

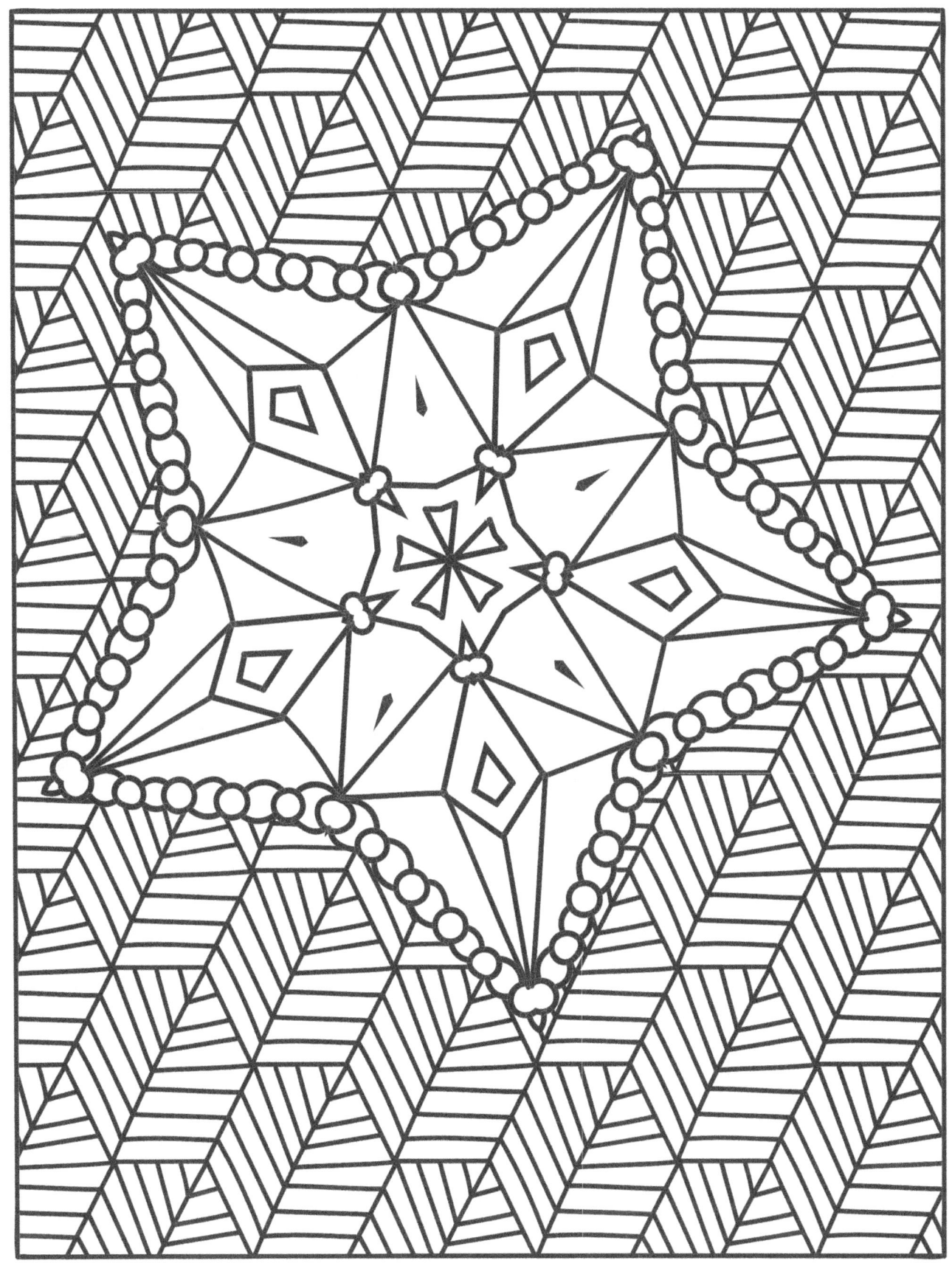

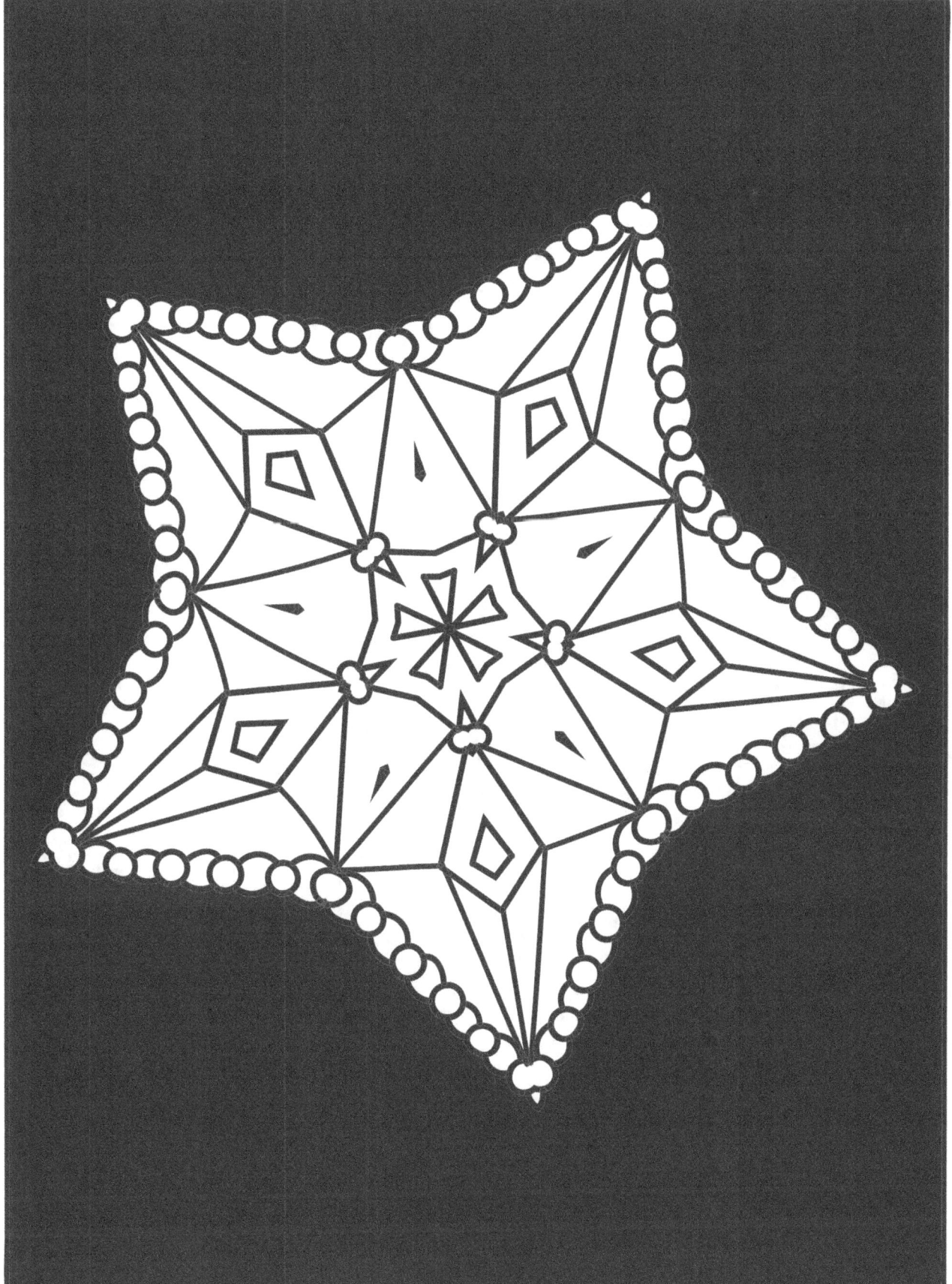

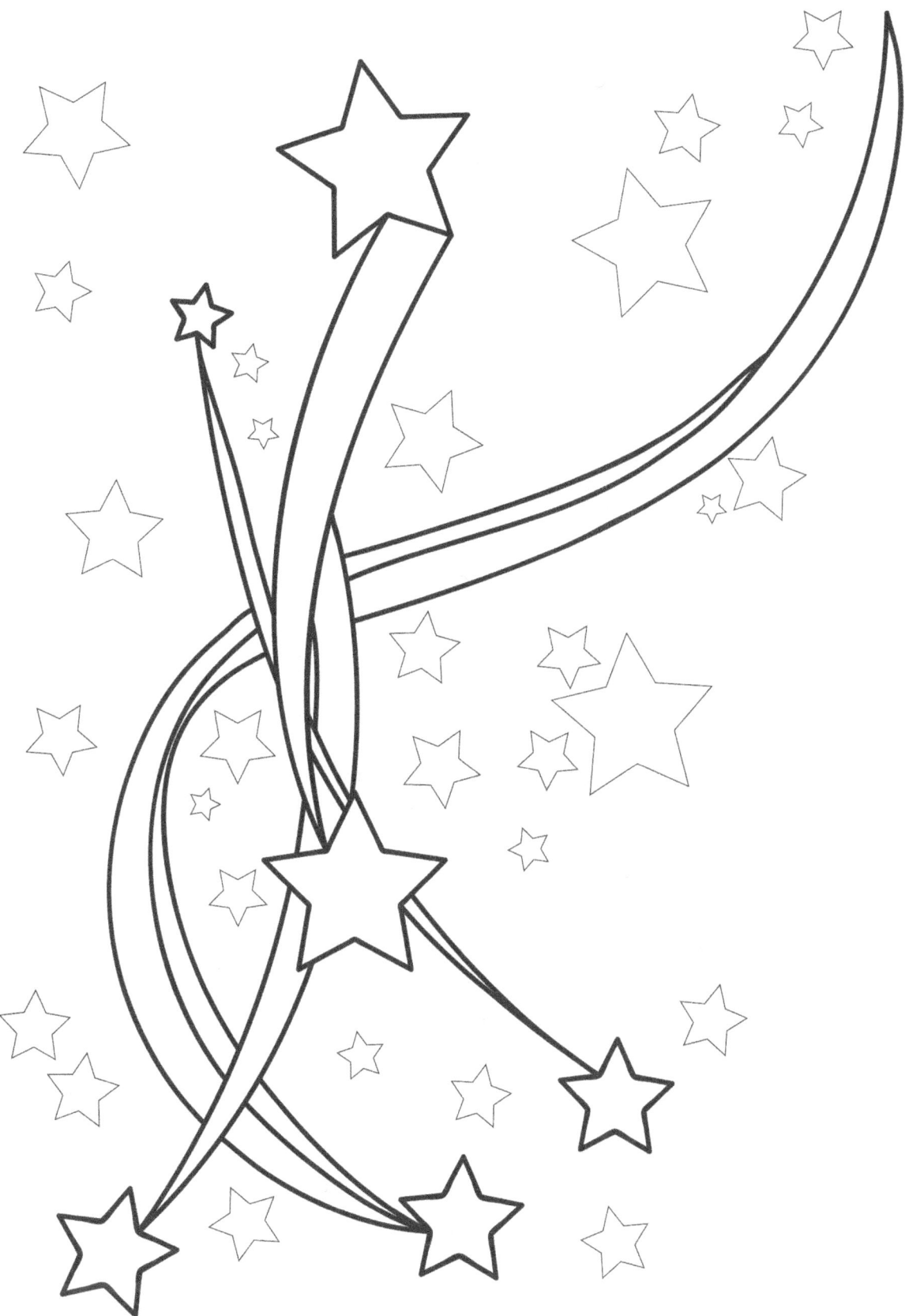

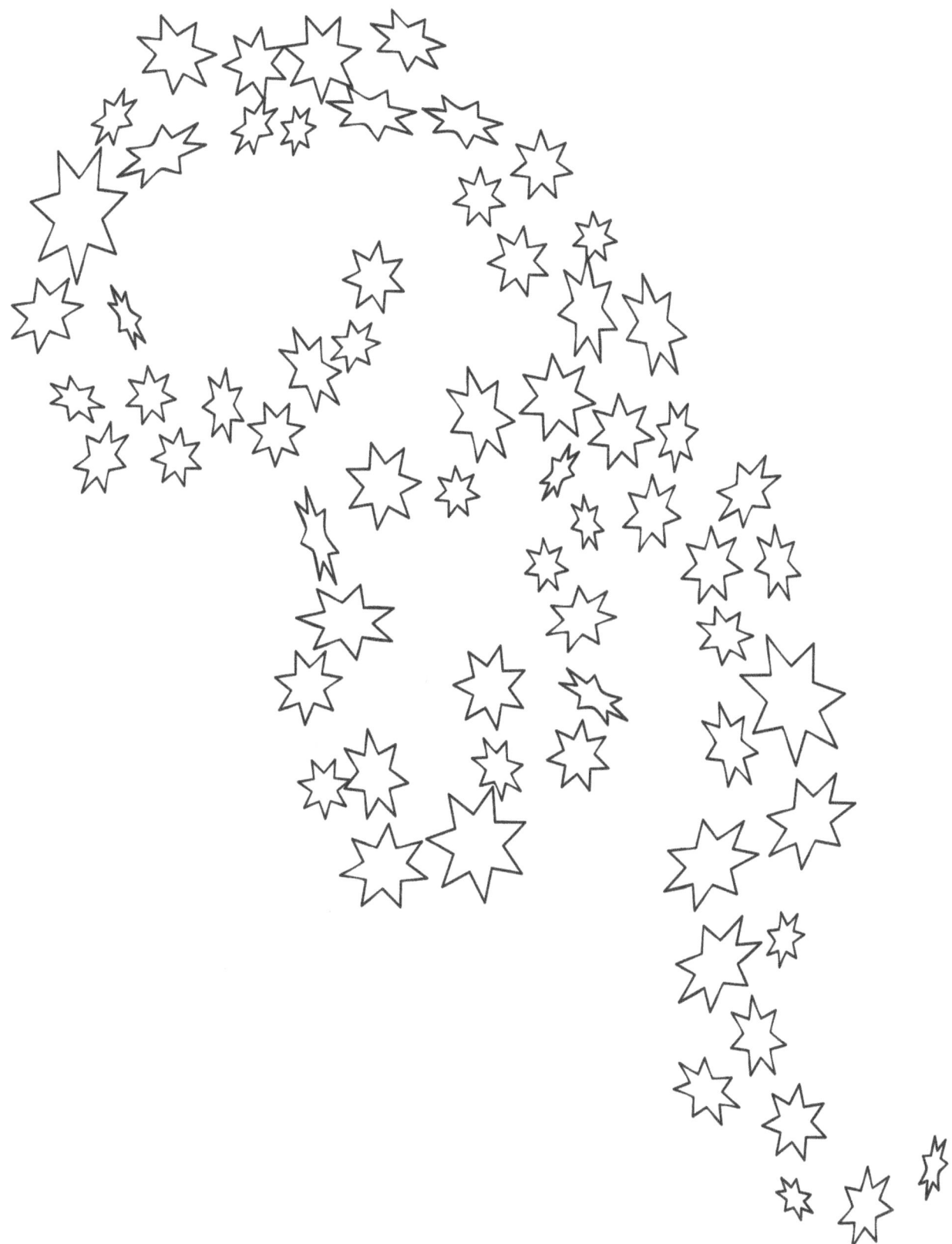

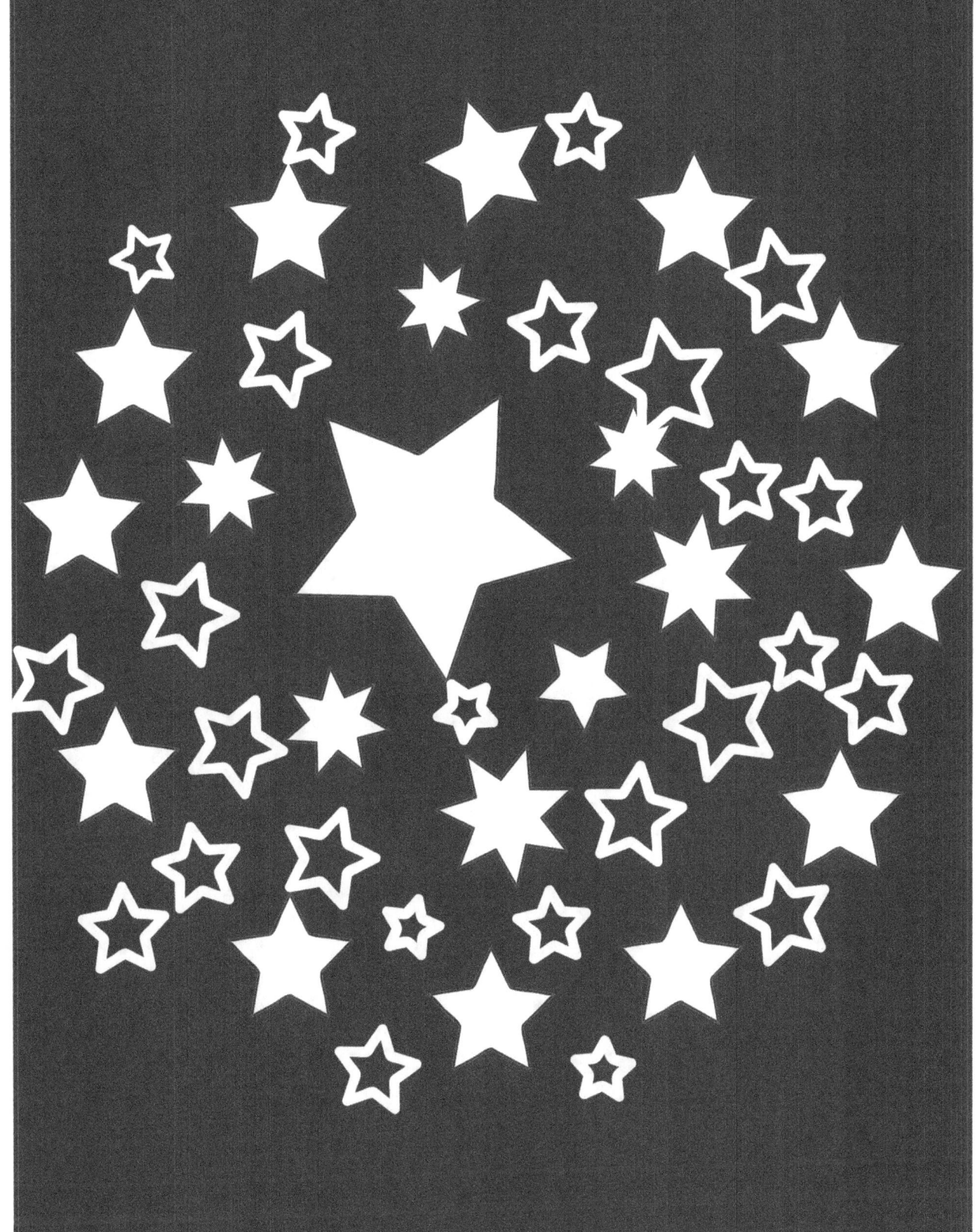

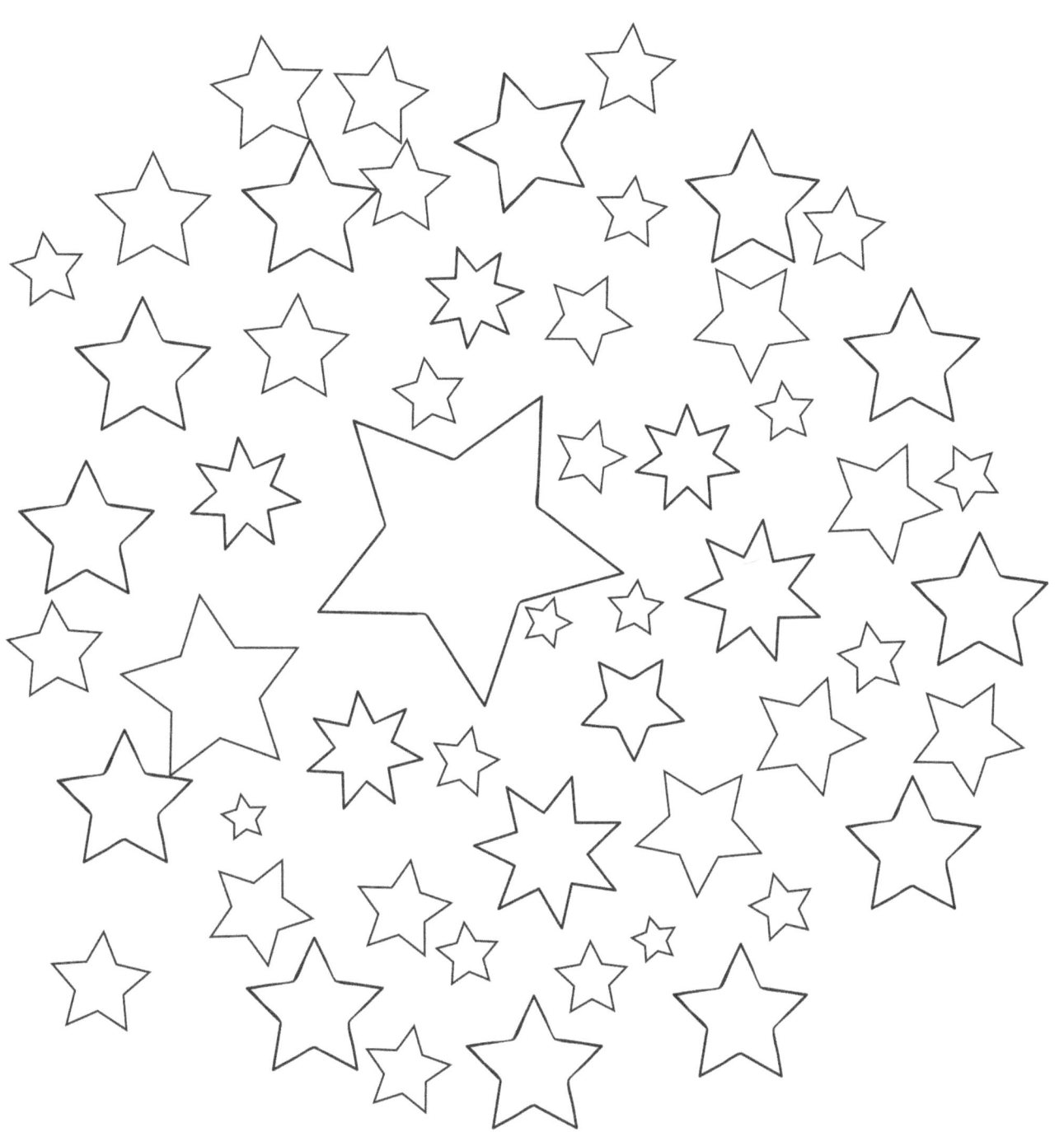

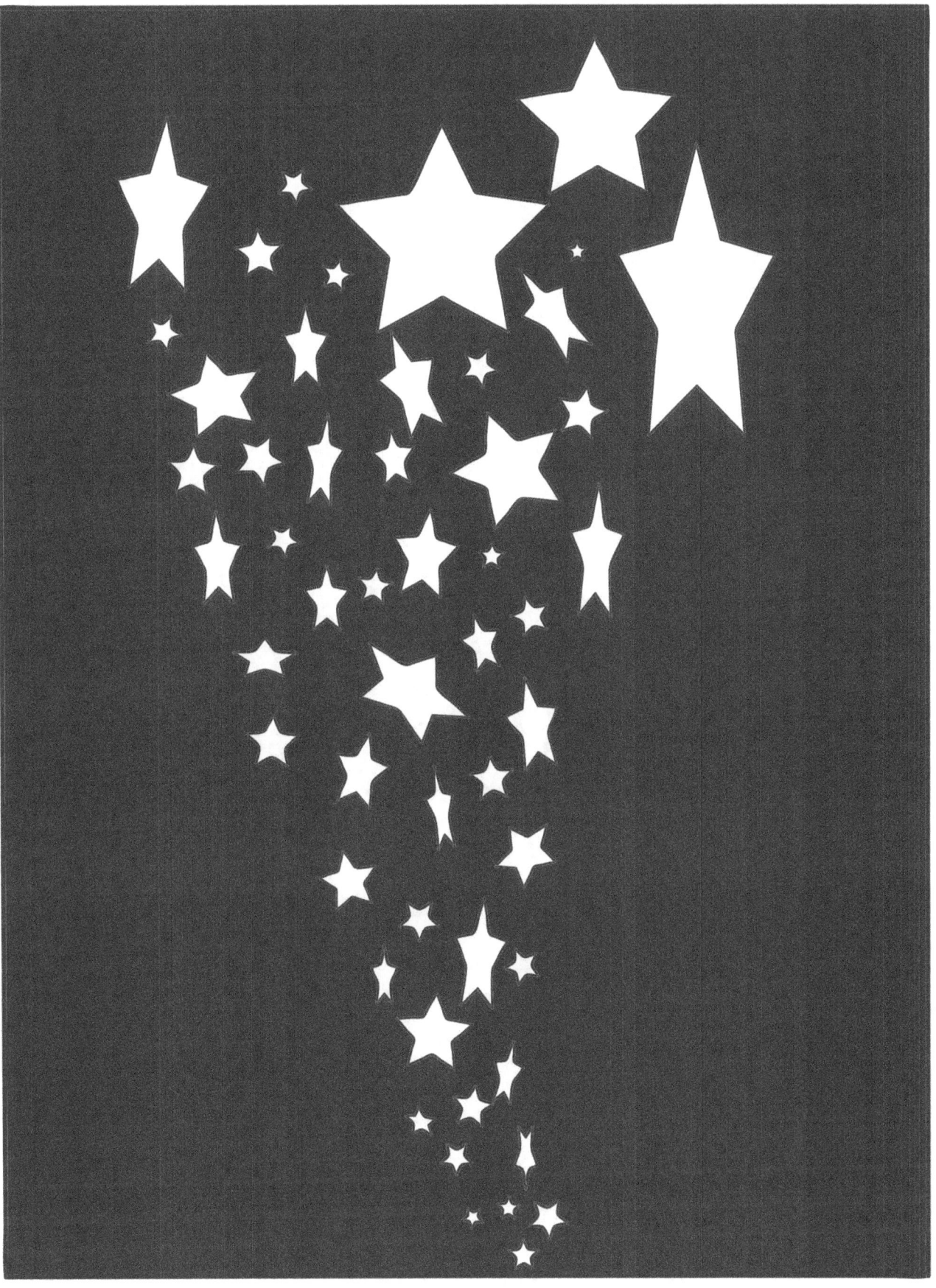

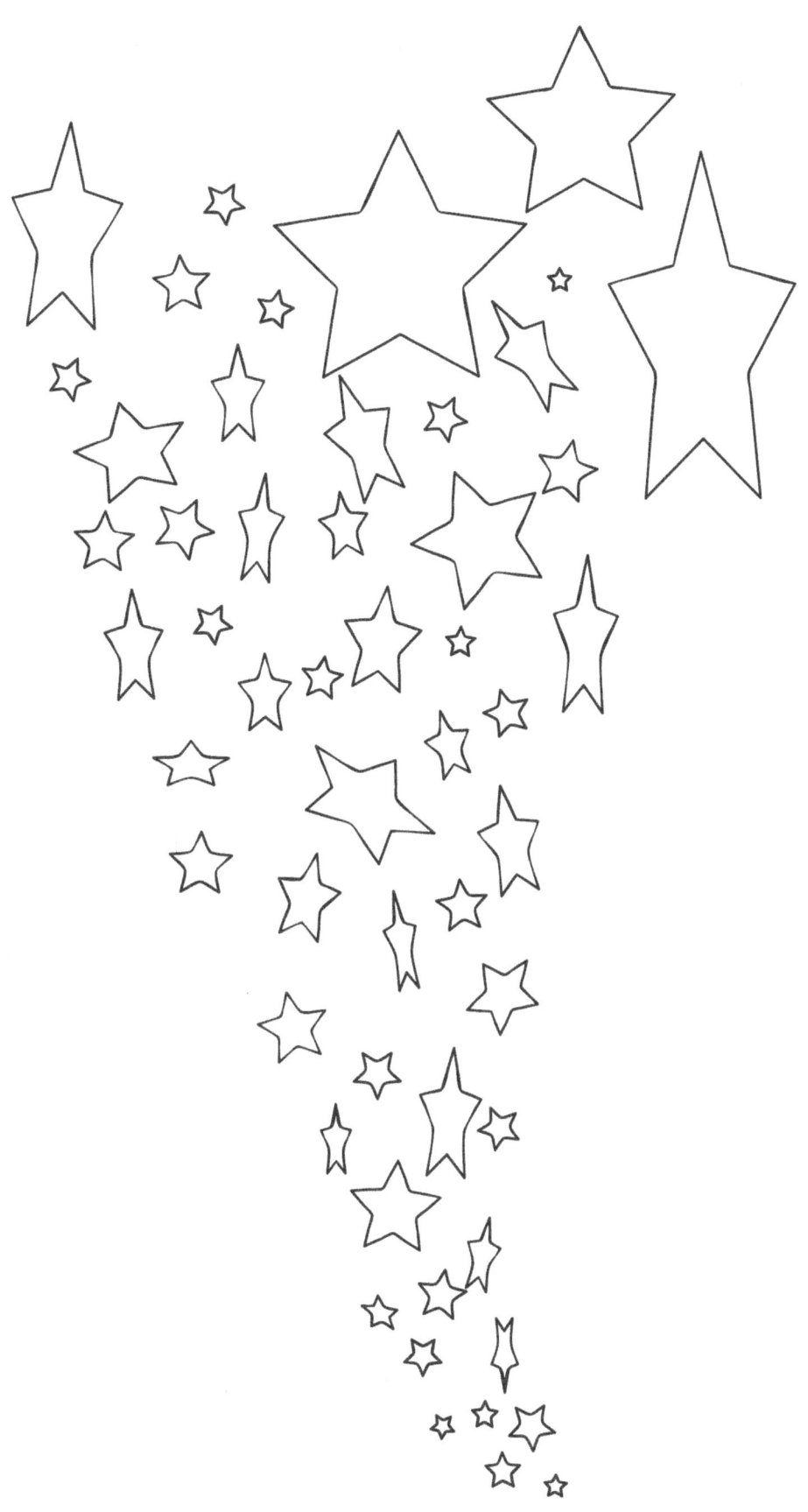

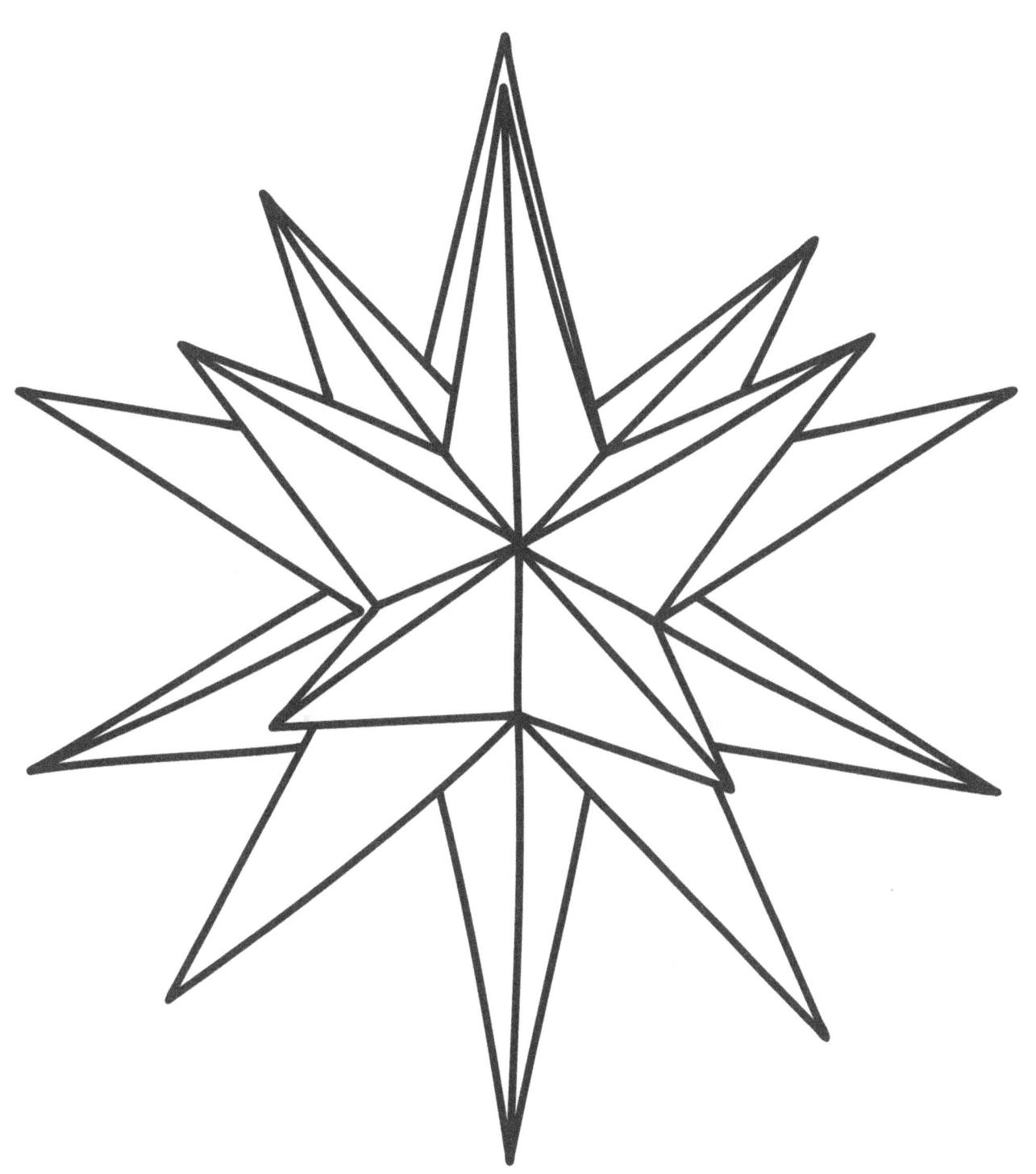

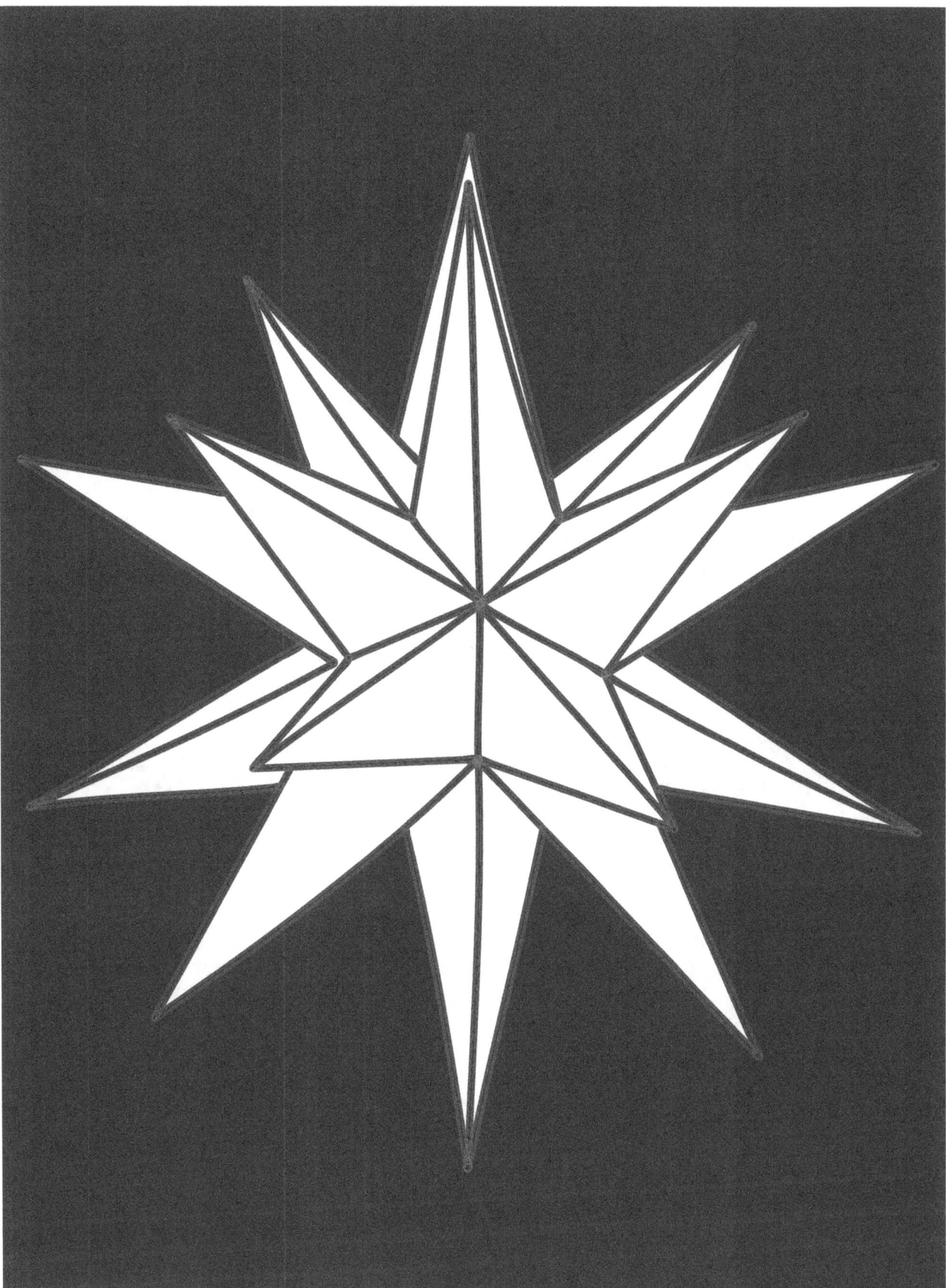

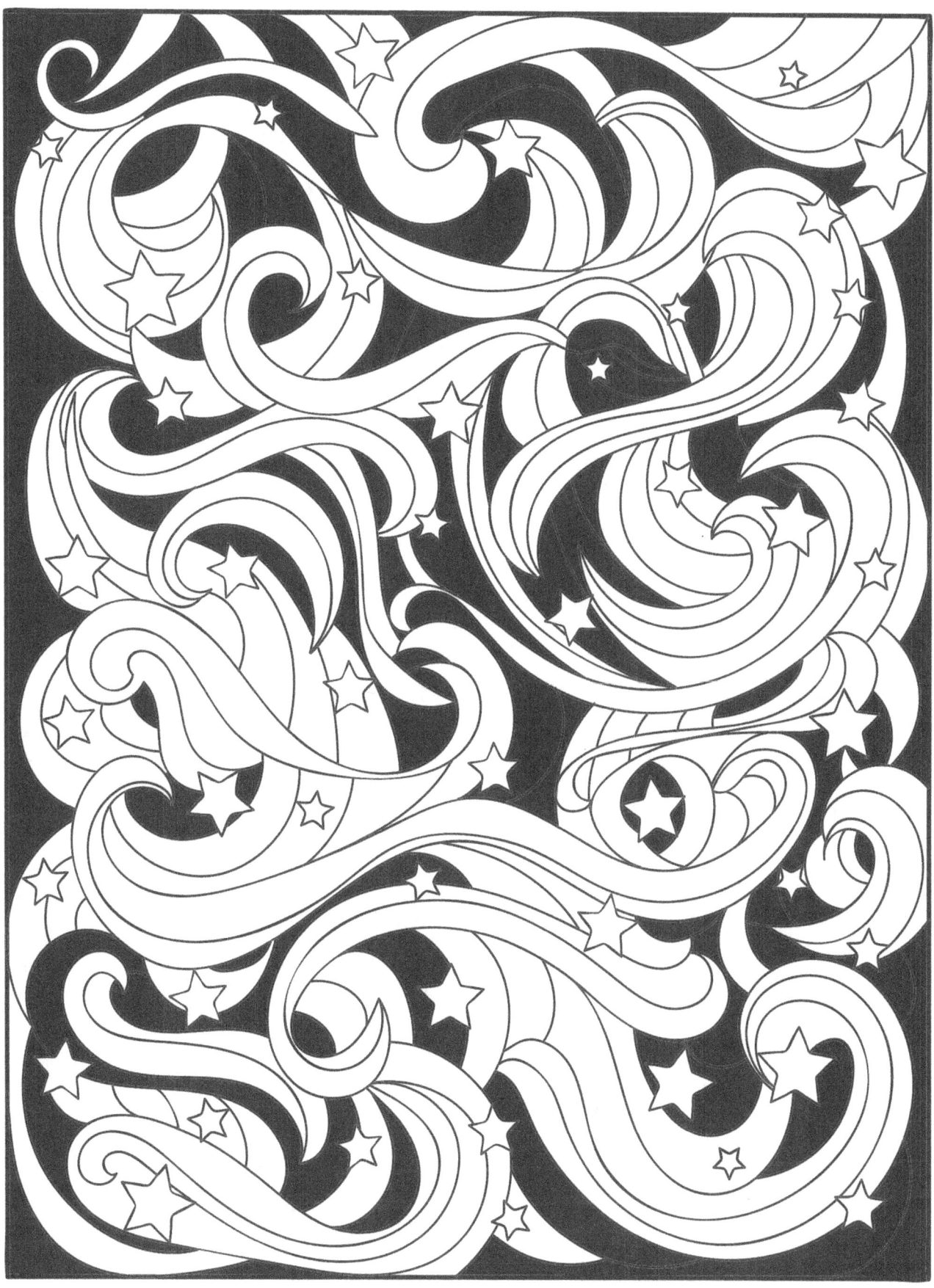

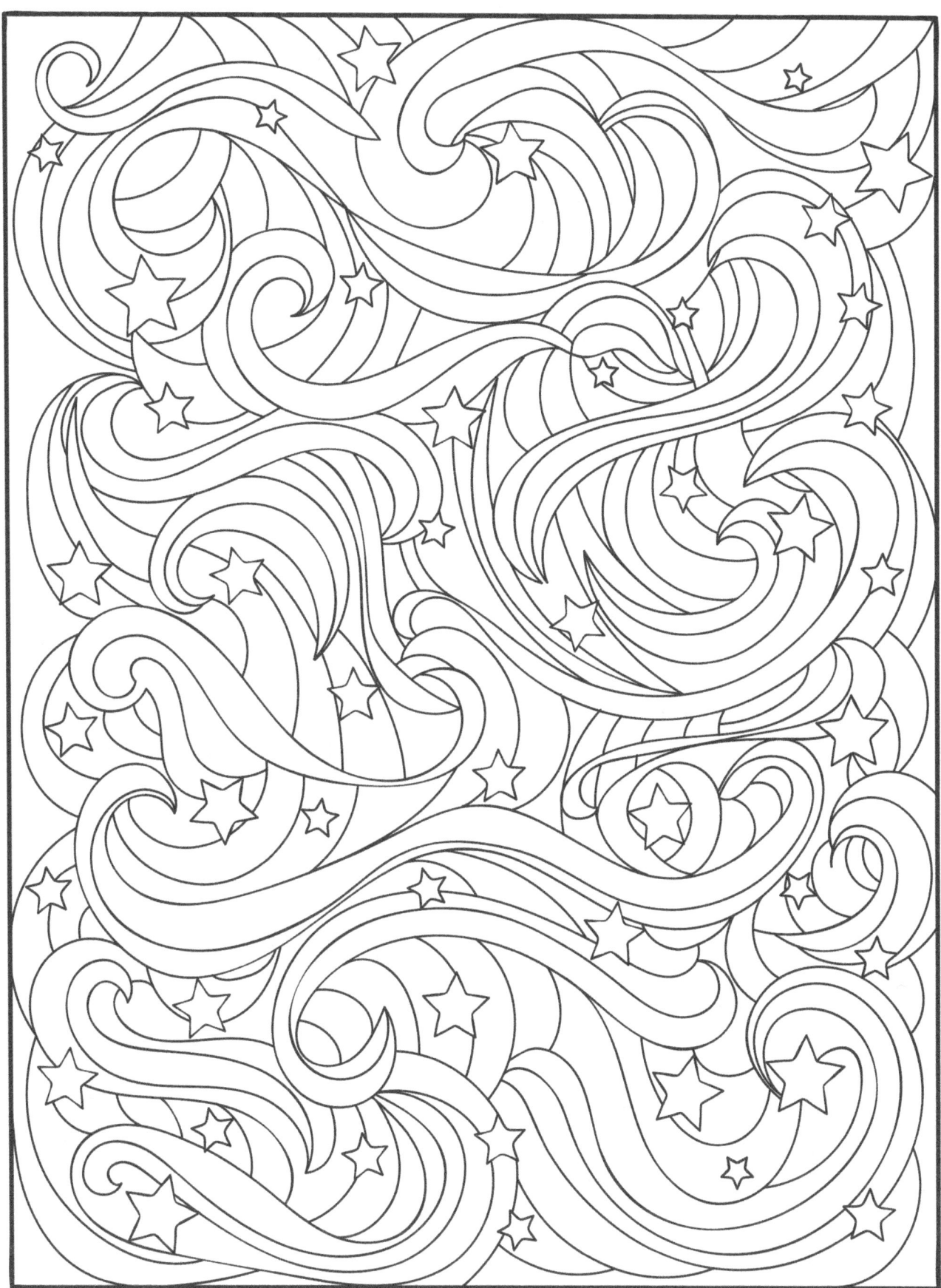

COLOR TEST PAGE

COLOR TEST PAGE

www.ingramcontent.com/pod-product-compliance
Lightning Source LLC
Chambersburg PA
CBHW082008230526
45468CB00023B/2899